15.95 Crabtree

516
KAI

D0622579

FEB 0 5 2009

What shape is it?

Bobbie Kalman

🌱 **Crabtree Publishing Company**

www.crabtreebooks.com

Created by Bobbie Kalman

For Crystal Sikkens, with thanks.
It is fun hunting down images with you!

Author and Editor-in-Chief
Bobbie Kalman

Editors
Reagan Miller
Robin Johnson

Photo research
Crystal Sikkens

Design
Bobbie Kalman
Katherine Kantor
Samantha Crabtree (cover)

Production coordinator
Katherine Kantor

Illustrations
All illustrations by Katherine Kantor except:
Barbara Bedell: page 15
Bonna Rouse: page 23

Photographs
© BigStockPhoto.com: page 12 (bottom)
© ShutterStock.com: front cover, pages 1, 3, 6 (bottom),
    7 (bottom), 8, 9 (bottom), 11, 13, 16 (top), 17, 19, 20,
    22 (shell and fish), 23, 24 (blocks)
Other images by Comstock, Corbis, Corel, Creatas, and
    Digital Vision

Library and Archives Canada Cataloguing in Publication

Kalman, Bobbie, 1947-
    What shape is it? / Bobbie Kalman.

(Looking at nature)
Includes index.
ISBN 978-0-7787-3320-1 (bound).--ISBN 978-0-7787-3340-9 (pbk.)

    1. Geometry in nature--Juvenile literature. 2. Shapes--Juvenile
literature. 3. Nature--Juvenile literature. I. Title. II. Series: Looking at
nature (St. Catharines, Ont.)

QA445.5.K34 2007   j508   C2007-904277-5

Library of Congress Cataloging-in-Publication Data

Kalman, Bobbie.
  What shape is it? / Bobbie Kalman.
    p. cm. -- (Looking at nature)
  Includes index.
  ISBN-13: 978-0-7787-3320-1 (rlb)
  ISBN-10: 0-7787-3320-3 (rlb)
  ISBN-13: 978-0-7787-3340-9 (pb)
  ISBN-10: 0-7787-3340-8 (pb)
  1. Shapes--Juvenile literature. 2. Geometry in nature--Juvenile
literature. I. Title. II. Series.

  QA445.5.K35 2008
  516'.15--dc22
                                          2007027238

Crabtree Publishing Company

www.crabtreebooks.com   1-800-387-7650

Copyright © **2008 CRABTREE PUBLISHING COMPANY.** All rights reserved. No part of this publication may be reproduced, stored in a retrieval system or be transmitted in any form or by any means, electronic, mechanical, photocopying, recording, or otherwise, without the prior written permission of Crabtree Publishing Company. In Canada: We acknowledge the financial support of the Government of Canada through the Book Publishing Industry Development Program (BPIDP) for our publishing activities.

Published in Canada
Crabtree Publishing
616 Welland Ave.
St. Catharines, Ontario
L2M 5V6

Published in the United States
Crabtree Publishing
PMB16A
350 Fifth Ave., Suite 3308
New York, NY 10118

Published in the United Kingdom
Crabtree Publishing
White Cross Mills
High Town, Lancaster
LA1 4XS

Published in Australia
Crabtree Publishing
386 Mt. Alexander Rd.
Ascot Vale (Melbourne)
VIC 3032

Contents

Shapes in our world

Everything in our world has a shape. Shapes are made with lines. Some shapes have **straight** lines. Some shapes have **curved** lines. Which two shapes are in this orange? Find these shapes on page 5.

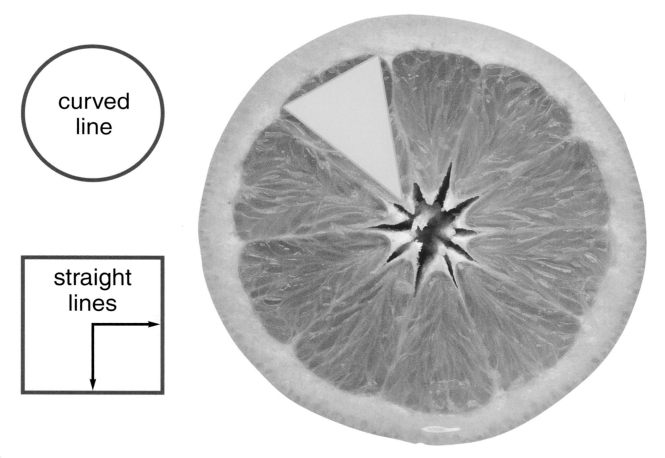

curved line

straight lines

Do you know these shapes?
They are all around you.
You can find them outdoors
and in your home.

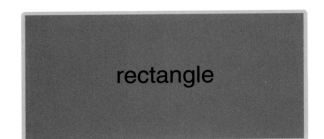

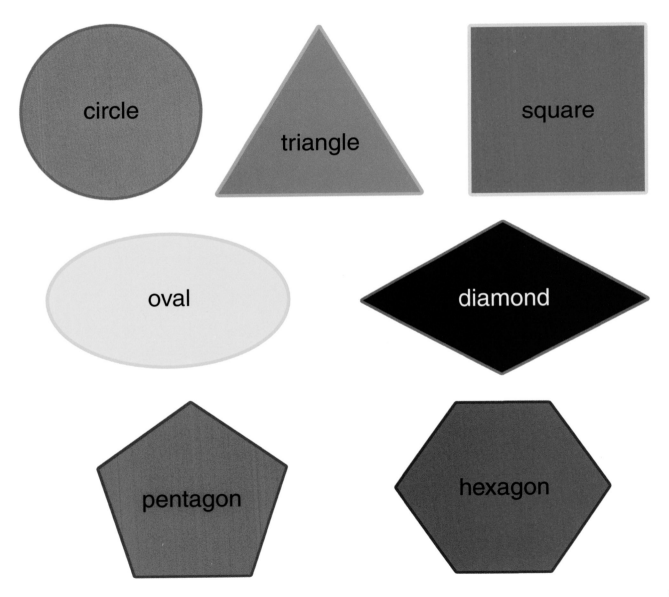

rectangle

circle

triangle

square

oval

diamond

pentagon

hexagon

Tons of triangles

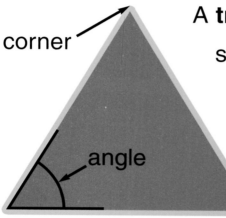

corner

angle

A **triangle** is a shape with three sides. A triangle has three **corners** and three **angles**. A corner is made by two lines that come together. Inside each corner, there is an angle.

The **fins** and nose of this ray have triangle shapes.

Many things in our world look like triangles. Some foods have triangle shapes. Strawberries are shaped like triangles. Some leaves are shaped like triangles.

How many triangles are in the wings of this butterfly? (See page 23.) Find five things in or near your home that have triangle shapes.

Four sides

A **square** is a shape with four sides. Each side is the same **length**. The tiles on this floor are squares. A square has four corners and four angles. Count the corners in each room of your home. How many corners are in your home?

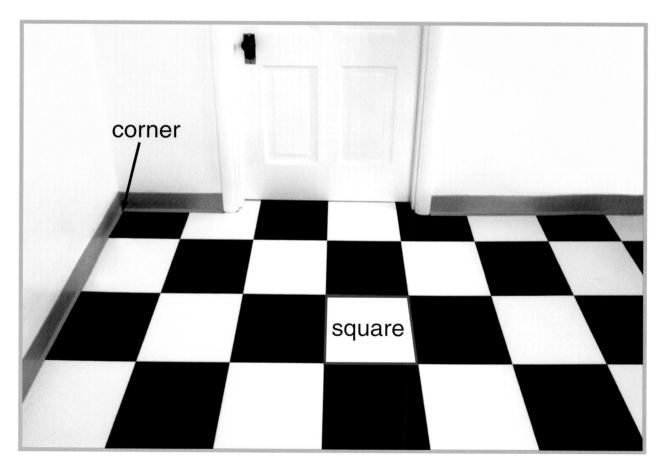

corner

square

A **rectangle** also has four sides. A rectangle is not the same as a square, however. A square has four sides that are the same length. A rectangle has two long sides and two short sides.

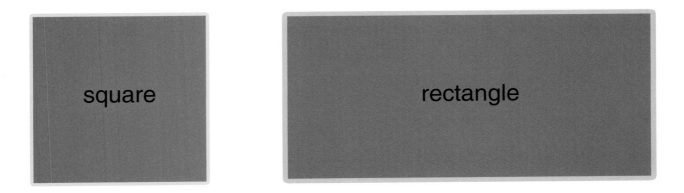

square

rectangle

This turtle has many rectangles on its shell. How many rectangles can you count?

Diamond shapes

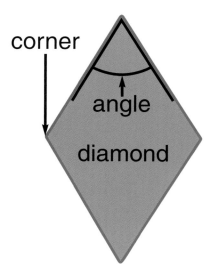

corner

angle

diamond

Diamonds have four sides, four corners, and four angles. The angles of diamonds are different from the angles of squares or rectangles. The body of this leaf mantis forms a diamond. What shape is the mantis's head? What shapes are its eyes?

Snakes are covered in **scales**. This picture shows a snake's scales up close. What is the shape of each scale?

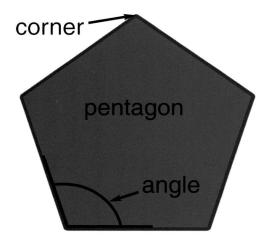

corner

pentagon

angle

Five sides

A **pentagon** has five sides and five corners. It also has five angles. The shape of this stingray is a pentagon.

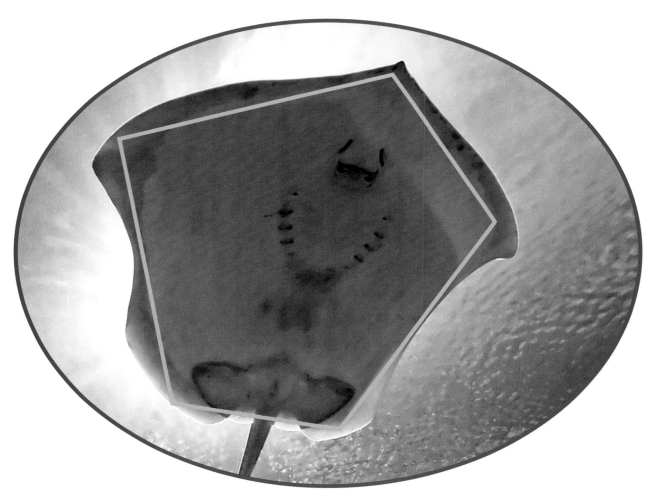

This sea star has a **star** shape. A star shape is made of five triangles with a pentagon in the center. When you draw a line around the outside of the star shape, you make another pentagon.

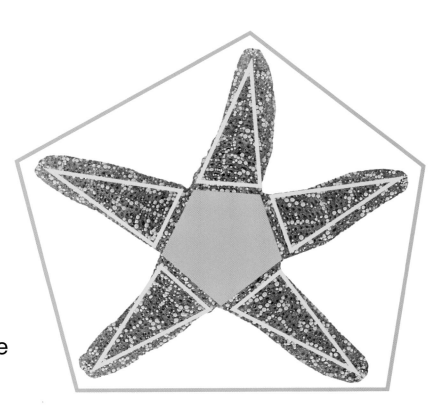

This picture shows a flower. How many pentagons can you see in the flower's center?

13

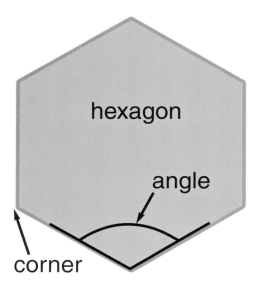

hexagon

angle

corner

Six sides

A shape that has six sides is called a **hexagon**. Hexagons have six corners and six angles, too. Bees live in **beehives**. Beehives are full of hexagons.

You can make your own beehive. Trace this circle. Then trace all the shapes inside onto a piece of paper. Make at least three circles. Be sure you trace all the lines.

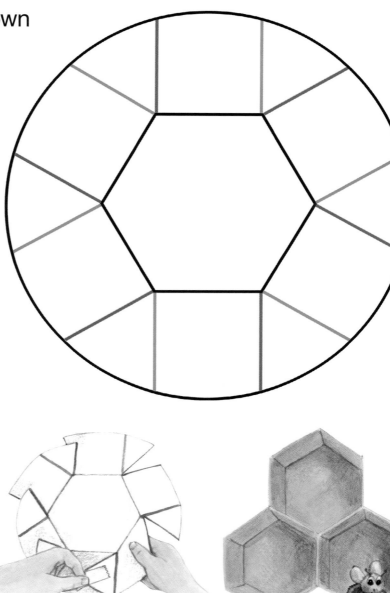

Cut out the circle. Cut along the red lines.

Fold along the blue lines. Tape down the folded flaps.

Paint your beehive orange.

Circles are round

A **circle** is a round shape. A circle is made using a curved line. It does not have straight lines. A circle has no sides. It has no corners or angles. The sun is a big circle.

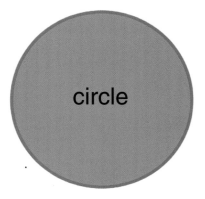

circle

Earth

Many things in our world are not flat. The Earth, sun, and moon are not flat like cookies. They are like balls. Circles that are round like balls are called **spheres**.

moon

The Earth is a sphere. The sun and the moon are spheres, too.

sun

17

Are these circles?

Ovals are like circles, but ovals are not round. The pictures on this page show oval shapes. How are ovals different from circles?

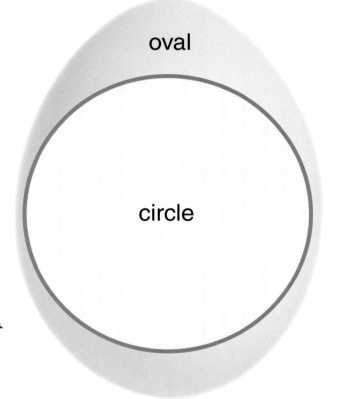

Ovals are like circles that have been stretched. An egg has an oval shape. These grapes are ovals, too.

18

Do these flowers
have circle shapes?
No. These flowers
have oval shapes.

This turtle's
shell also has
an oval shape.

3-D shapes

square

A square is a shape with four sides. The four sides are the same length. A **cube** is made up of squares. These blocks are cubes. Just as spheres are not flat circles, cubes are not flat squares. Shapes that are not flat are called **3-D shapes**. 3-D is short for **three-dimensional**.

cube

Each side of a cube is a square. Find a cube in your home or classroom and count how many sides it has. Did you count six?

This seashell has a **cone** shape. A cone is like a triangle, but it is also round. An ice-cream cone has a cone shape, too.

cylinder

A tree trunk is round, but it is not a sphere. It is not an oval. A tree trunk has a **cylinder** shape. A cylinder is a 3-D shape.

What is its shape?

Now that you know some shapes, take a look around you. There are shapes everywhere! What shapes do you see in these pictures?

What shapes can you see in this fish's body? How many circles are there? How many triangles are there?

Is this seashell a circle? It looks like a circle, but if you look closely, you can see that the curved lines do not meet. This round shape is called a **spiral**.

circle

spiral

22

Can you count the rectangles in this house? I cannot. There are more than 100! The door, windows, steps, boards, shingles, and the sides of the house are all rectangles. How many rectangles are in the door?

Find square, circle, oval, diamond, and triangle shapes in the picture above.

Answer to page 7:
There are six triangles on the butterfly. Four small triangles make up two big triangles.

Words to know and Index

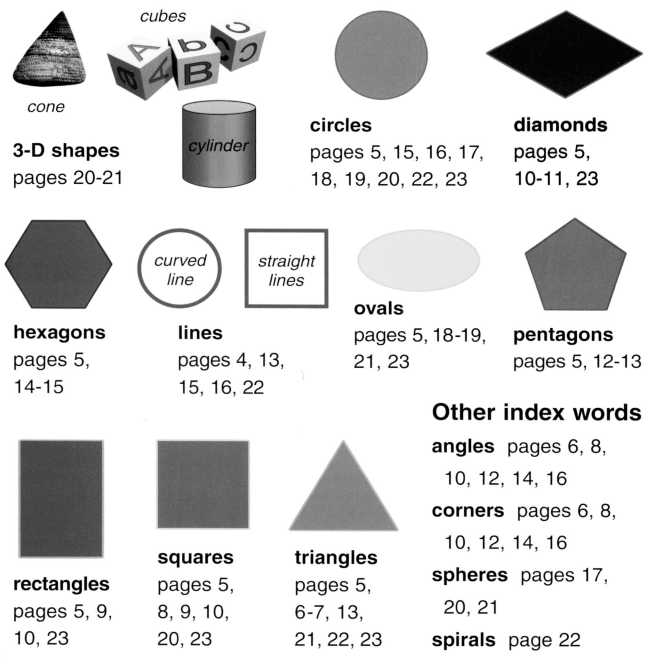

cubes

cone

3-D shapes
pages 20-21

cylinder

circles
pages 5, 15, 16, 17,
18, 19, 20, 22, 23

diamonds
pages 5,
10-11, 23

hexagons
pages 5,
14-15

curved
line

straight
lines

lines
pages 4, 13,
15, 16, 22

ovals
pages 5, 18-19,
21, 23

pentagons
pages 5, 12-13

rectangles
pages 5, 9,
10, 23

squares
pages 5,
8, 9, 10,
20, 23

triangles
pages 5,
6-7, 13,
21, 22, 23

Printed in the U.S.A.